SAVE THE ANIMALS

ELEPHANT ORPHANS

W9-AAV-285

Clare Hibbert

PowerKiDS
press.

New York

Published in 2015 by
The Rosen Publishing Group, Inc.
29 East 21st Street, New York, NY 10010

Library of Congress Cataloging-in-Publication Data

Hibbert, Clare, 1970- author.
 Elephant orphans / Clare Hibbert.
     pages cm. — (Save the animals)
 Includes bibliographical references and index.
 ISBN 978-1-4777-5896-0 (pbk.)
 ISBN 978-1-4777-5900-4 (6 pack)
 ISBN 978-1-4777-5898-4 (library binding)
 1. David Sheldrick Wildlife Trust—Juvenile literature.
 2. African elephant—Infancy—Kenya—Juvenile
 literature. 3. African elephant—Reintroduction—
 Kenya—Juvenile literature. 4. African elephant—Effect
 of poaching on—Kenya—Juvenile literature. 5. Wildlife
 conservation—Kenya—Juvenile literature. 6. Wildlife
 reintroduction—Kenya—Juvenile literature. I. Title.
 QL737.P98H53 2015
 599.67'4—dc23

                          2014026398

First published in 2015 by Franklin Watts
Copyright © Arcturus Holdings Limited

Editor: Joe Harris
Picture researcher: Clare Hibbert
Designer: Tokiko Morishima

Picture credits: all images Eric Baccega/Nature PL
except pages 2–3: Pete Oxford/Nature PL and pages
5 (bg) and 14-15 (bg): Shutterstock. Cover image:
Pete Oxford/Nature PL

Manufactured in the United States of America

CPSIA Compliance Information: Batch #CW15PK: For Further Information contact
Rosen Publishing, New York, New York at 1-800-237-9932

CONTENTS

ELEPHANT NURSERY

The grasslands of Kenya in East Africa are home to a very special organization — the David Sheldrick Wildlife Trust Nairobi Elephant Nursery. It was set up to look after orphaned young elephants and rhinos.

Elephant and rhino orphans cannot survive on their own in the wild. The Nairobi Elephant Nursery rescues orphans that are found in the national park where it is based. It raises the animals and nurses them back to health. When they are old enough, they are released back into the park. The park is Tsavo East National Park, one of Kenya's oldest and largest national parks.

KENYA

Tsavo East National Park

Nairobi

The wildlife trust that runs the nursery was set up more than 35 years ago. It is named in honor of David Sheldrick, the first warden of Tsavo East National Park. David studied the elephants in the park. He and his wife Daphne also rescued elephants in danger. Since the trust has been set up, it has hand-raised more than 150 infant elephants.

THREATS TO ELEPHANTS

The main threats to wild elephants are habitat loss and poaching. Elephants are losing their habitat as people clear the bush for villages, towns and farms. Drought (when rains fail) can be a problem, too.

Poachers kill elephants for their tusks, which are made of ivory. Since 1990 it has been illegal to trade ivory, but that does not stop some people buying and selling it. "Subsistence hunters" spear elephants for their meat. Farmers sometimes shoot elephants that damage their crops.

Fact File: Elephant Populations

Both African and Asian elephants are threatened. In the 1930s, there were probably between three and five million elephants living across Africa. Today there are as few as 600,000. There are only around 40,000 Asian elephants.

Poachers set traps called snares to catch elephants. The snared elephant may die of starvation before the poacher returns to saw off its tusks. The good news is that the wildlife trust has seven teams patrolling the bush and removing snares. Sometimes they remove as many as 1,000 snares in a couple of days.

This baby elephant has been injured by a spear.

MOTHER'S MILK

When a mother elephant is poached, she often leaves behind a helpless baby. As a baby mammal, an elephant calf needs to drink milk to survive. Without its mother to feed it, an elephant orphan would soon die in the wild.

One of the most important and time-consuming jobs at the Nairobi Elephant Nursery is feeding the elephants. Some orphans come to the center when they are only a week or two old. These newborns are fed on demand around the clock. They need to feed little and often because their tummies are small and they digest their food very quickly. They drink up to 35 pints (20 liters) of milk a day!

As the calves grow up, the keepers gradually stretch out the time between feeds. Soon, the babies feed only once every three hours. A calf would normally feel very safe when it snuggles up to its mother to feed. The keepers try to give the orphans the same feeling of safety. They set up a feeding station that is like a pretend mom. It has a cozy blanket strung up between sturdy posts (the "legs").

The feeding station is covered with a blanket.

9

FOOD SUPPLIES

Preparing food is a big part of the keepers' jobs. They serve up a special type of milk drink that they have perfected over the years. The magic ingredient is coconut milk. Its sugars are easy to digest and give the youngsters plenty of energy!

When the calves are five months old, the keepers start adding oatmeal porridge to their milk. It contains the vitamins and minerals the babies need to grow up strong. As the youngsters start to eat plant food, their milk feeds are cut back to three a day. However, they will still need milk up to the age of five.

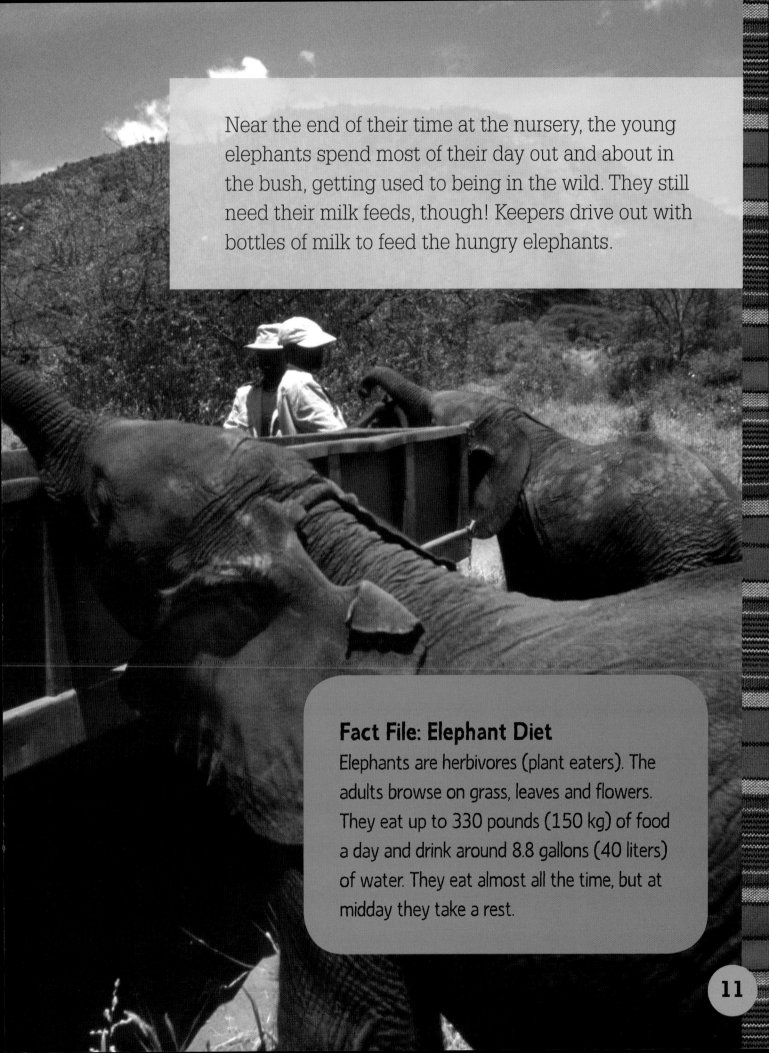

Near the end of their time at the nursery, the young elephants spend most of their day out and about in the bush, getting used to being in the wild. They still need their milk feeds, though! Keepers drive out with bottles of milk to feed the hungry elephants.

Fact File: Elephant Diet

Elephants are herbivores (plant eaters). The adults browse on grass, leaves and flowers. They eat up to 330 pounds (150 kg) of food a day and drink around 8.8 gallons (40 liters) of water. They eat almost all the time, but at midday they take a rest.

DUST BATHS

Taking a bath is an important part of the orphans' daily routine — it happens in the middle of the morning and then again at the end of the afternoon. These are no ordinary baths, though. The elephants roll around in mud or dust!

The elephants don't look very clean after a mud bath, but that is not the point. The mud acts as a sunscreen. It protects the animals' skin from burning in the hot African sun. The mud also helps to keep the elephants cool. As water in the mud dries out in the heat, it cools their skin. The elephants' wrinkles make the cooling effect last longer. Water trapped in the wrinkles takes more time to dry out.

The elephants use the rich, red dust out in the bush as a sunscreen, too. It also has another purpose – it puts off the insect parasites that like to set up home on a baby elephant's hide! Without a mother to show them what to do, the orphans must learn from each other. The keepers also help by digging up spadefuls of dust and throwing it over the calves.

In the wild, calves learn from their mothers.

A NEW ARRIVAL

The wildlife trust sends out teams of vets to find and treat animals that have been injured by poaching. Sometimes these units pick up orphaned elephants. They bring them to the nursery. They are often in poor health when they arrive.

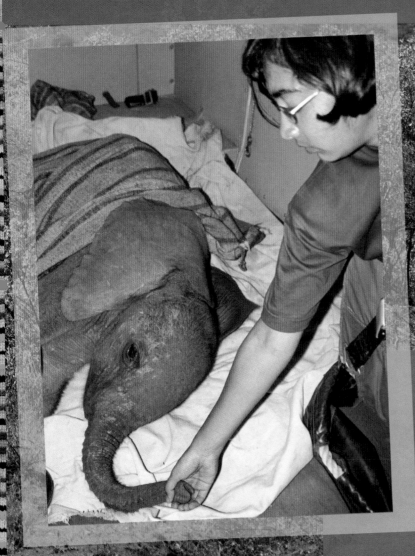

Sometimes the trust hears of an animal that has been separated from its herd. A calf may be trapped in a waterhole or lost on someone's farmland. The trust arranges for the calf to be brought in by truck or plane.

Fact File: Mobile Vet Unit

The mobile vet unit is a team of vets who drive around the bush in all-terrain vehicles. They can respond quickly to sightings of injured animals. They rescue animals caught in snares or, if necessary, end their suffering quickly and painlessly. The vets also keep an eye on the spread of diseases.

Dehydration (lack of water) is the most urgent problem. The emergency team gives a new calf the fluids it needs right away. The animal may also be near starvation or have bullet, arrow, or spear wounds. Soon it will be in a place of safety. The nursery's trained staff will be able to help it recover.

HEALTH CHECKS

The keepers at the Nairobi Elephant Nursery nurse the orphans back to health. Newly-arrived orphans often have bloated stomachs and thin faces. They have not been able to find enough food, or the right food — this is called malnutrition. With regular feeds at the nursery, they soon recover.

The keepers carefully check the orphans' health and keep track of changes. The calves are regularly weighed. If they are not putting on weight, the animals can be given more frequent feeds. They may also be put on a special diet. Weight loss can be the first sign of disease. The keepers move animals that show signs of sickness to a separate area. That is the best way to stop diseases from spreading.

The keepers examine the calves' teeth. Elephants need these to grind up tough plant foods. If they have not been able to find enough to eat, the calves' tusks and teeth may not have grown properly. The keepers examine the orphans' eyes, too. If a calf is blind, it will probably stay in captivity all its life. It would not manage to survive out in the wild.

HEALING TOUCH

Elephants are social animals. Youngsters are used to being part of a herd. They would normally live in close-knit family groups led by adult females. When they are orphaned, the loss of their social group can be very upsetting for them.

Elephant herds are made up of adult females, along with all their offspring. Female calves stick with the herd for all their lives, but males go off on their own at the age of 12 to 15 years. Within the herd, the elephants strengthen their family bond with lots of touching.

At the nursery, the keepers do not want the orphans to miss out on the physical contact that they would have had from their elephant family. The keepers give the calves plenty of strokes and pats and cuddles – and the elephants seem to respond with signs of affection, too.

Fact File: Feelings

Elephants are known for their great intelligence and their amazing memories. Researchers have noticed that herd members visit "graveyards" — the places where their dead ancestors' bones are. They touch and stroke the skulls with their trunks. Are they paying their respects to the dead?

ELEPHANT FRIENDS

The elephants at the nursery become playmates. The friendships that they share help to prepare them for life in a wild herd. They communicate with each other through noises, body language, smell, and touch.

The elephants show their affection by touching each other with their trunks, ears, tusks, feet, tails or even their whole bodies! Their muscular trunks are incredibly sensitive and flexible. One end is split into two "fingers" that can poke and grasp. Elephants smell through their trunks, too, and will remember a buddy's unique scent for their entire lifetimes.

To comfort new arrivals, the other elephants sometimes poke their trunks through the stable bars and stroke them. When they are playing, the calves might tangle their trunks together in a sort of "hug!" They also press trunks. At the age of around two, the elephants move from the nursery to a new area, called a rehabilitation center. They seem to recognize old friends from back at the nursery.

OFF FOR A WALK

While they are in the nursery, one of the highlights of the elephants' routine is their daily walk. The keepers take the youngsters out into the bush. The outings get them used to the sights, sounds, and smells of life out in the wild.

The orphans head out every day. Some may have bad memories of the bush, but they are part of a group now. That makes them feel safe again. These walks will help to get them ready for the next stage in their journey.

Fact File: Rehabilitation

"Rehabilitation" means getting ready for normal life. The trust has two rehabilitation centers. Once elephants move to these centers, they spend all day out in the bush. Sometimes they stick close to their keepers and sometimes they wander further away. However, they return to the same fenced area each night.

Walks teach the youngsters useful things, such as where the waterholes are. They sometimes come into contact with wild elephants. The walks happen through the year. On chilly mornings, a keeper might stop and light a fire, giving the youngsters a chance to pause and explore.

PLAYTIME

Like all baby animals, young elephants like to play. They have fun with each other and with their keepers, too. Playing together is a way of strengthening friendships. It also allows the elephants to practice adult behaviors.

The elephants sometimes play-fight, especially the young males. As adult bull elephants, males will compete for females by fighting. For now, the calves are just pretending. They try out the right body language and learn to have better control over their clumsy feet, trunks and ears! They show when they are ready to play by doing a special head waggle.

Play stops the elephants from getting bored. They might kick a ball around or splash about in a waterhole. They are exercising both their bodies and their brains! Water is great fun – and playing in it is a way to keep cool, too. The calves suck up lots of water in their trunks and then squirt it over each other!

BEDTIME

Like all animals, elephants need more sleep as infants than adults. During sleep, they can take a rest from thinking about their daily lives at the center. Their brains and bodies can carry out important repair work. When they wake again, they will be ready for another busy day!

In the wild, infant elephants sleep snuggled close to their mother. At the nursery, the keepers provide this warmth and comfort. Each keeper sleeps in a different elephant's stable each night to make sure the animals see all the keepers as "family," not just one particular human.

A keeper eats his supper before going to bed.

When calves move to the rehabilitation center, their sleeping routine changes. The elephants need to start preparing for life in a herd in the wild. The animals do not sleep with the keepers. They all sleep together in the stockade instead.

Fact File: Wild Adults

Adult elephants do not need very much sleep at all — just four hours in every 24. They sleep for a few hours just before dawn and again during the hottest part of the day. Adults usually sleep standing up, ready to move away quickly if they hear a predator.

SPREADING THE WORD

In the decades since it was set up, the Wildlife Trust has made an important difference. Looking after orphaned elephants and rhinos is just a small part of that. The trust helps to protect many different wildlife species and their habitat in East Africa.

The Wildlife Trust is improving the situation for all the wildlife in Tsavo East National Park. Its vets and anti-snaring teams help other animals, not only the elephants. The trust is also working hard to show people how important conservation (protecting wildlife) is.

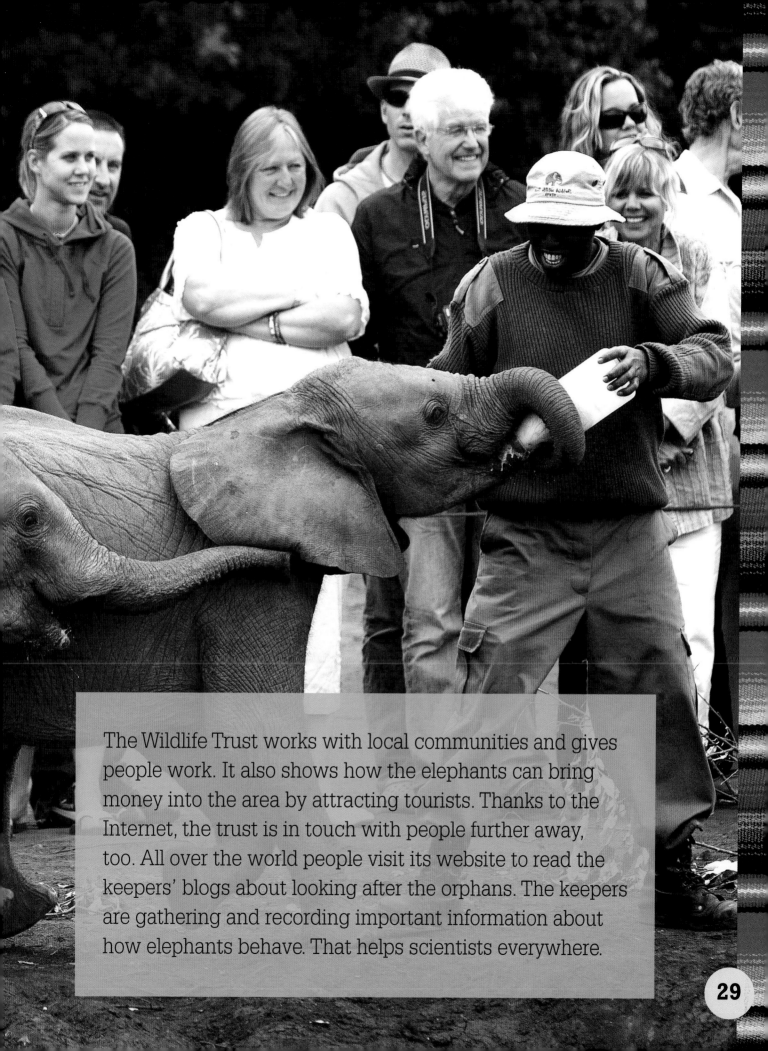

The Wildlife Trust works with local communities and gives people work. It also shows how the elephants can bring money into the area by attracting tourists. Thanks to the Internet, the trust is in touch with people further away, too. All over the world people visit its website to read the keepers' blogs about looking after the orphans. The keepers are gathering and recording important information about how elephants behave. That helps scientists everywhere.

GLOSSARY

BROWSE To feed on grass or leaves.

BUSH Wild, uncultivated land, especially savannah.

CAPTIVITY The situation of being kept in a place such as a zoo, animal rescue center or someone's home, rather than living in the wild.

CONSERVATION Protecting and keeping for the future.

DEHYDRATION Lacking fluids.

EVAPORATE To turn from a liquid to a vapor.

FLUIDS Liquids that can be drank.

HABITAT The place where an animal or plant lives.

HERBIVORE An animal that eats plants for food.

ILLEGAL Against the law.

MALNUTRITION Poor health because of not having had enough food.

NATIONAL PARK An area where the land is protected by law so that it stays wild.

ORPHANED Having lost its parents. In elephant society, where mothers raise the calves within the herd, a baby who has lost its mother counts as "orphaned."

PARASITE An animal or plant that survives by living off another animal or plant.

PATROL To travel over an area regularly to check that all is well.

POACHING Stealing or killing animals illegally.

PREDATOR An animal that survives by hunting, killing, and eating other animals.

REHABILITATION Being prepared to live a normal life.

SAVANNAH African grassland, with few or no trees.

SNARE A trap for catching animals.

STARVATION Suffering or dying from lack of food.

SUBSISTENCE HUNTER Someone who hunts and eats animals as a way to stay alive.

THREATENED Describes a species of animal on its way to becoming endangered (at risk of dying out completely) in the future.

WARDEN An official who is in charge of something, such as a national park.

WATERHOLE A place where animals regularly go to drink.

FURTHER INFORMATION

FURTHER READING

100 Facts: Elephants by Camilla de la Bedoyere (Miles Kelly Publishing, 2009)

Animal Families: Elephant by Tim Harris (Wayland, 2014)

Animal Lives: Elephants by Sally Morgan (QED Publishing, 2014)

Animals on the Edge: Elephants by Anna Claybourne
(Bloomsbury Childrens, 2012)

The Elephant Scientist by Caitlin O'Connell and Donna M. Jackson
(Houghton Mifflin Harcourt, 2011)

Elephants by Laura Marsh (National Geographic Kids, 2014)

WEBSITES

Due to the changing nature of Internet links, PowerKids Press has developed an online list of websites related to the subject of this book. This site is updated regularly. Please use this link to access the list:

www.powerkidslinks.com/sta/elep

INDEX